ALFRED'S
BASIC ADULT
PIANO
COURSE
LESSON BOOK   LEVEL THREE

WILLARD A. PALMER   MORTON MANUS   AMANDA VICK LETHCO

Correlated materials to be used with Adult Lesson Book, Level 3:

Title	Start on page
Adult Theory Book 3	4

A CD  (34929) is available, and includes a full piano recording of each song.

The goal of Level Three of Alfred's Basic Adult Piano Course is to provide a very flexible and highly enjoyable presentation that will allow the student to progress smoothly and easily, without gaps, toward playing in some of the more advanced keys, as well as playing some of the great masterworks of piano literature.

This book is divided into four sections:

1. A REVIEW OF OLD KEY SIGNATURES (but with some new concepts added).

2. NEW KEY SIGNATURES AND CONCEPTS.

3. "JUST FOR FUN" SECTION. Pieces in this section are for relaxation and amusement. They may be played whenever the student wishes.

4. "AMBITIOUS" SECTION. This section is for the student who is willing to devote a little extra effort toward learning some of the great masterworks that require a bit of additional practice. They are within the capabilities of anyone who has completed the previous books of this series and the first two sections of this book.

The book closes with a Dictionary of Musical Terms. Students who wish to review all the scales and the primary chords of each key may use pages 90–94 of Alfred's Basic Adult Piano Course, Level TWO.

The authors are confident that the selection of material for this book will provide the student with a great variety of pleasing music to play, since it includes many familiar favorites, along with a variety of effective original keyboard compositions.

Alfred

Contents

A SUPER-SPECIAL SORTA SONG!

This book begins with a piece that is just for fun. It reviews the key of C major, and you will find it easy to play. There are more "JUST FOR FUN" pieces in this book on pages 62–73. You may play from that section of the book any time you wish.

Moderate & relaxed

Play eighth notes in long-short pairs.

Willard A. Palmer

Optional 2nd verse: Light and easy, play it bright and breezy,
And this super-special song will make you smile like the "Mona Leezy."
It's all right, it never can be wrong,
Because it's such a super-special sorta song!

And the beat is so neat, *etc.*

You are now ready to begin Adult THEORY BOOK 3 (#11745).

1. neat,
2. play,

And the notes are so nice,
And the rhy- thm's so right,

That I'm tap- pin' my feet,
I could play it all day!

And I'm play- in' it
I could play it all

twice!
night!

It's a pleas- ure to

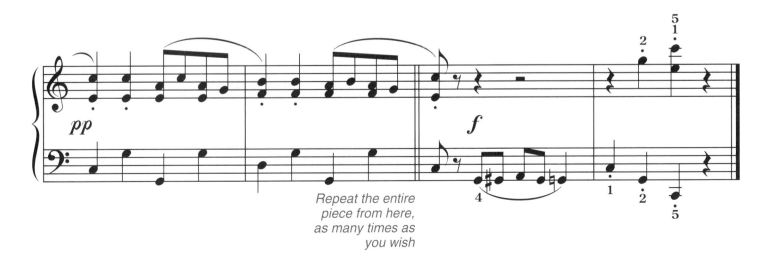

*Repeat the entire
piece from here,
as many times as
you wish*

CALYPSO RHUMBA

A STUDY IN OVERLAPPING PEDALING

KEY OF C MAJOR
Key Signature: no #, no ♭.

Andante moderato

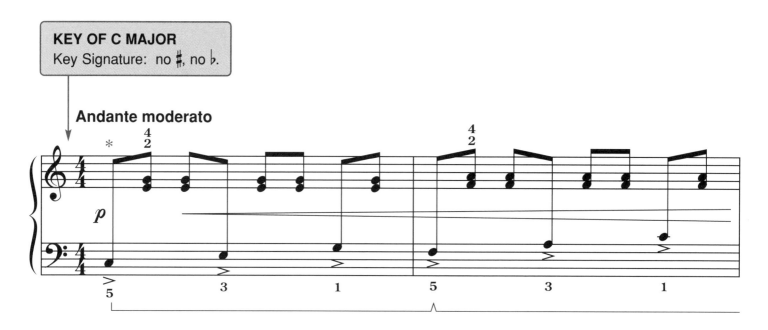

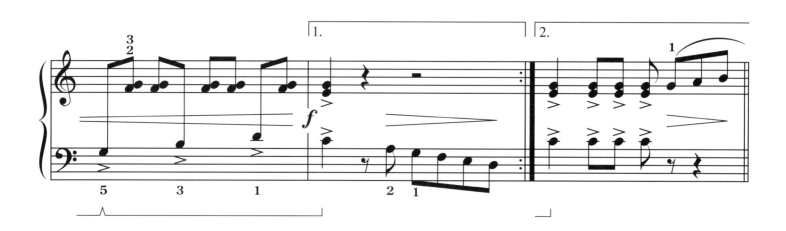

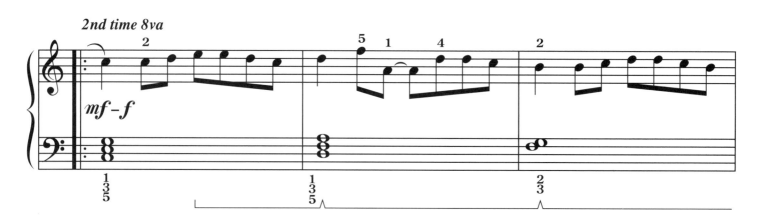

*Play eighth notes evenly!

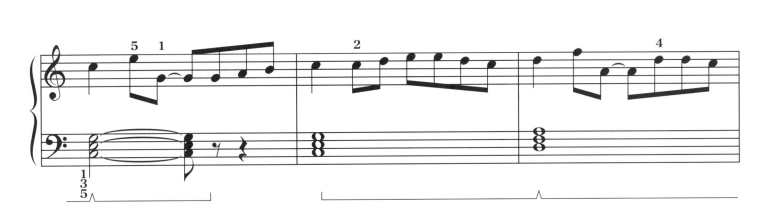

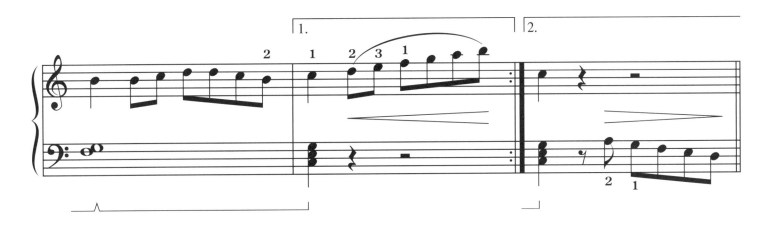

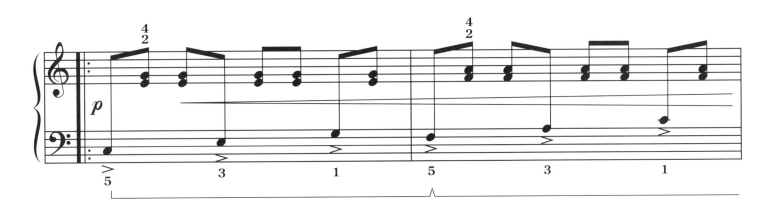

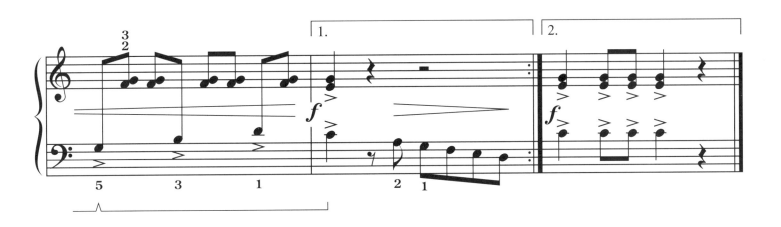

8

FANDANGO

The *FANDANGO* is a lively Spanish dance with three beats per measure. It is usually based on this chord progression:

KEY OF A MINOR*
Key Signature: no #, no ♭.

***Reminder:** A MINOR is the *relative minor* of the key of C MAJOR. Both keys have the same key signature.

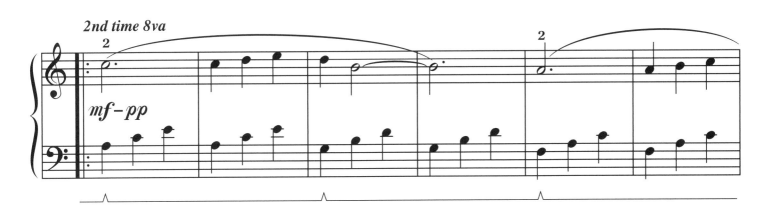

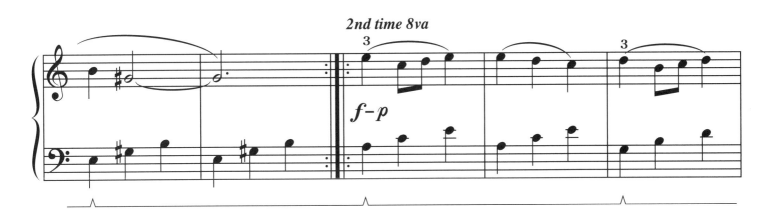

D. C. al Fine

MODERN SOUNDS

This piece begins with the RH and LH moving up and down the keyboard in thirds. All the thirds are fingered with the 2nd and 4th fingers. RH and LH 2s are on neighboring white keys.

In the second section only the RH plays thirds.
The LH plays fifths with 5 and 1.

This piece shows how thirds and fifths can be used to produce very modern sounds.

This piece combines the use of the relative minor and major keys.

D. C. al Fine

Alberti Bass

This style of LH accompaniment takes its name from the 18th-century Italian composer, Domenico Alberti, who used it extensively in his keyboard music. It consists of broken chords played as follows:

This style was frequently used by almost all the "classical" composers, including Haydn, Mozart, Clementi and Beethoven. The following two examples of *Alberti bass* are from Mozart's *Sonata in C Major,* K. 545, and Clementi's *Sonatina in D Major,* Op. 36, No. 6.

W. A. Mozart

Allegro

Allegro con spirito

Muzio Clementi

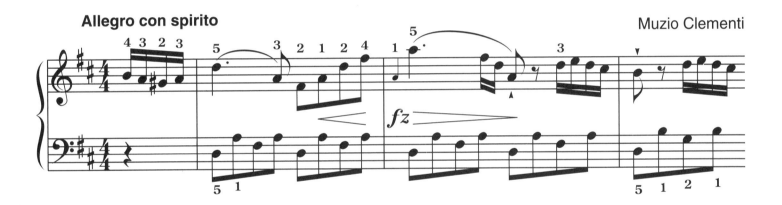

The first line of the music below shows a basic **I–IV–V⁷** progression in C major. The second line shows the corresponding Alberti bass. Practice each line several times before playing *SERENADE* (pages 12 and 13). Be sure to play the eighth notes evenly.

Chord Progression

Alberti Bass

SERENADE from String Quartet, Op. 3, No. 5

Play the eighth notes *evenly!*

Franz Joseph Haydn

*OPTIONAL: The LH may be played one octave higher in the first and second lines.
When doing so, play the RH G half note (measure 4) as an eighth note.

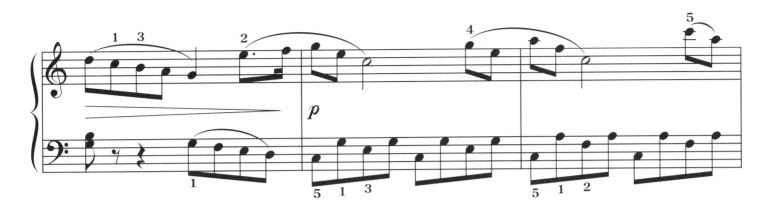

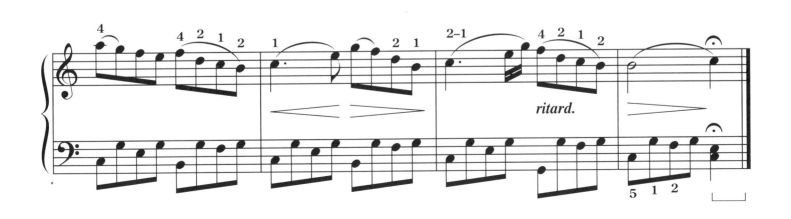

A New Style of Bass

This style of accompaniment is often used in popular as well as classical music.

Begin with this as a warm-up:

Play the following exactly the same as the above, but HOLD the first note of each group of four notes:

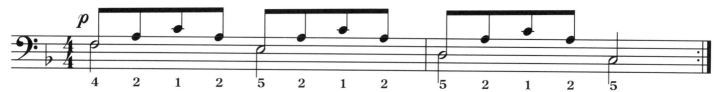

A VERY SPECIAL DAY

Willard A. Palmer

KEY OF F MAJOR
Key Signature: 1 flat (B♭)

Andante moderato

1. This is a
ver - y spe - cial day
ver - y spe - cial day
I'm of - fer - ing to you,
I'd love for you to share.

The day I dream of when I pray
It's such a ver - y spe - cial way
That wish - es may come
To show how much we

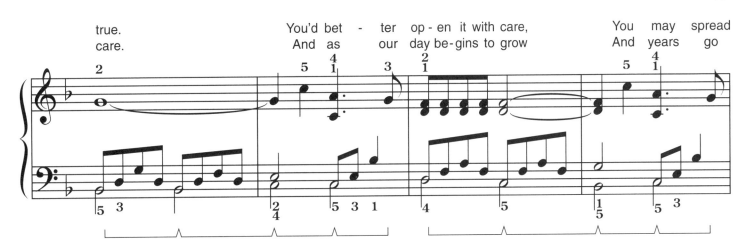

true.
care.
You'd bet - ter op - en it with care,
And as   our day be-gins to grow
You may spread
And years go

sun-shine ev-'ry- where!
by I'm sure we'll know
As you may guess,
That on this   day
It's full of
We're glad we

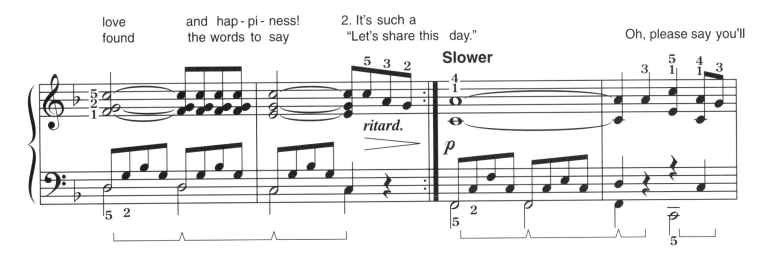

love
found
and hap - pi - ness!
the words to say
2. It's such a
"Let's share this day."
Oh, please say you'll

Slower

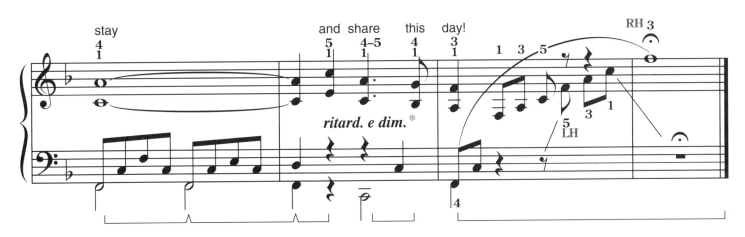

stay
and share this day!
Oh, please say you'll

*ritardando and diminuendo

The Diminished Seventh Chord

The DIMINISHED SEVENTH chord may be formed by lowering each note of the DOMINANT SEVENTH (V^7) chord one half step, except the root, which remains the same.

IMPORTANT! The interval between each note of a diminished seventh chord is a *minor* 3rd (3 half steps)!

Be sure to *spell* each chord correctly! The Gdim7 chord must not be spelled **G B♭ D♭ E**, even though the notes E and F♭ are ENHARMONIC (that is, they represent the same key on the piano). The interval from G to E is a 6th. The interval from G to F♭ is a 7th (in this case a *diminished* 7th).

In forming a Cdim7 chord, it is necessary to flat the note B♭. When a flatted note is flatted again, it becomes a DOUBLE FLAT, indicated by the sign ♭♭. In this case, the note must be called B♭♭, not A!

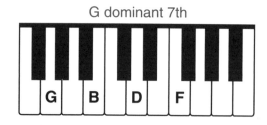
G dominant 7th

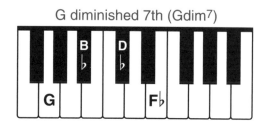
G diminished 7th (Gdim⁷)

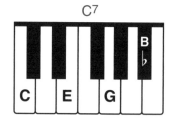
C⁷

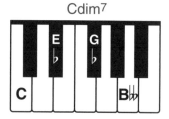
Cdim⁷

REMEMBER: When diminished 7th chords are properly spelled, one letter of the musical alphabet is skipped between each note. Use your SEVENTH CHORD VOCABULARY (Adult Lesson Book 2, page 46)!

Play a dim7 chord on each note of the CHROMATIC SCALE, beginning as shown below. Build each chord by adding 3 notes above the root, each 3 half steps apart. Play with RH using 1 2 3 5 on each chord. Repeat one octave lower with LH, using 5 3 2 1.

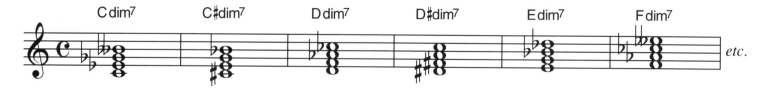

A Classy Rag

Circle all the broken diminished 7th chords before you play.

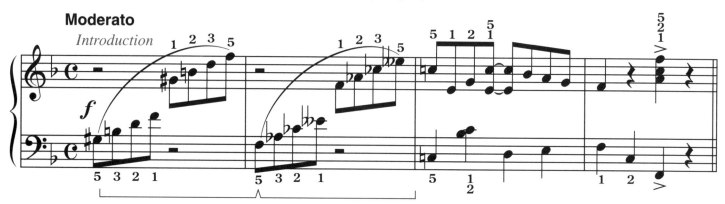

*OPTIONAL: Play the *Introduction* with both hands *8va* as an added ending (CODA) for the entire piece.

A Special Style of Pedaling

In the following piece, the pedal is applied only to the eighth notes played by the RH. These notes should be played with a clear legato touch, even though they are sustained by the pedal.

Observance of the two-part writing in the left hand results in the sustaining of the LH notes with the *fingers.* This is sometimes called *finger pedaling.* By combining LH finger pedaling with pedaled notes in the RH, a beautiful tone color is produced. This style of pedaling is often effective, especially in pieces constructed largely of broken-chord figurations.

PRELUDE IN D MINOR

KEY OF D MINOR*
Key Signature: 1 flat (B♭)

Muzio Clementi
from *Introduction to the Art
of Playing on the Pianoforte*

*REMINDER: D MINOR is the *relative minor* of the key of F MAJOR.

How many broken diminished 7th chords can you find in this piece?

Check the *spelling* of each diminished 7th chord.

NOTE: You may now wish to play *PRELUDE IN C MAJOR,* from J. S. Bach's *Well Tempered Clavier, Vol. 1,* found on pages 74–77, in the "AMBITIOUS" section of this book. The Bach prelude is especially effective when you use the same style of pedaling as is mentioned above.

THE STAR-SPANGLED BANNER

KEY OF B♭ MAJOR
Key Signature: 2 flats (B♭ & E♭)

Words by Francis Scott Key
Music by John Stafford Smith

Con spirito*

Con spirito means "with spirit."

 This sign means *tremolo*. Alternate the lower and upper note of the octave as rapidly as you can, keeping the wrist relaxed. (You may also just play the octave and hold it for the entire measure.)

SCENE FROM THE BALLET,
"SWAN LAKE"

Peter Ilyich Tchaikovsky (1840–1893) was a great Russian composer who found success in every musical medium, including symphonies, songs, opera, chamber music, instrumental and choral works, and ballet. There is no more popular large piano work than his famous *Concerto in B♭ Minor,* which American pianist Van Cliburn played when he won the International Piano Competition in Moscow in 1957. Tchaikovsky also gave the world its two most famous ballets: *The Nutcracker,* and *Swan Lake,* from which this scene is taken.

Tchaikovsky
adapted by P. M. L.

KEY OF G MINOR*
Key Signature: 2 flats (B♭ & E♭)

*REMINDER: G MINOR is the *relative minor* of the key of B♭ MAJOR.

meno mosso means "slower."

SCHEHERAZADE

Theme from the Third Movement
"THE YOUNG PRINCE AND THE YOUNG PRINCESS"

N. Rimsky-Korsakov

KEY OF G MAJOR
Key Signature: 1 sharp (F♯)

*Slide the thumb from D♯ to E, as smoothly as possible.

*The three notes of a sixteenth note triplet are played evenly, in the time of *one eighth note.*

Tempo primo* means "the first tempo," in this case, **Andante.

THEME FROM "THE UNFINISHED SYMPHONY"

Preparation: Play several times, counting aloud.

Moderato

Franz Schubert

*Play the C & D together with the side tip of the thumb.

*REMINDER: *sf (sforzando)* means suddenly louder on one note or chord. Here it applies to both RH and LH notes.

**OPTIONAL: You may play octaves in place of the tremolo, using half notes.

SPOOKY STORY

KEY OF E MINOR*
Key Signature: 1 sharp (F♯)

Andante moderato, mysteriously
VERY IMPORTANT: Play both hands one octave lower than written throughout!

Fine

*REMINDER: E MINOR is the *relative minor* of the key of G MAJOR.

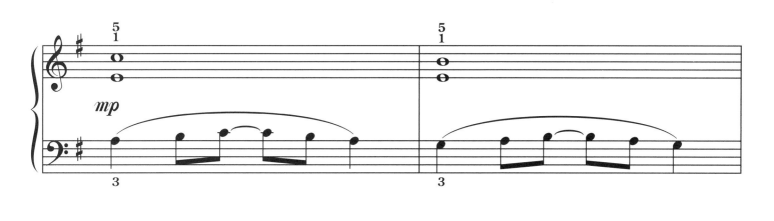

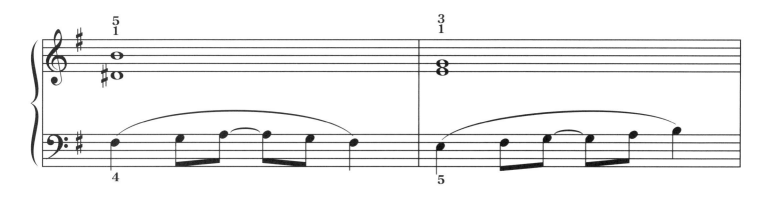

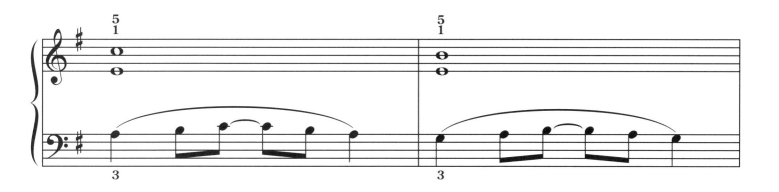

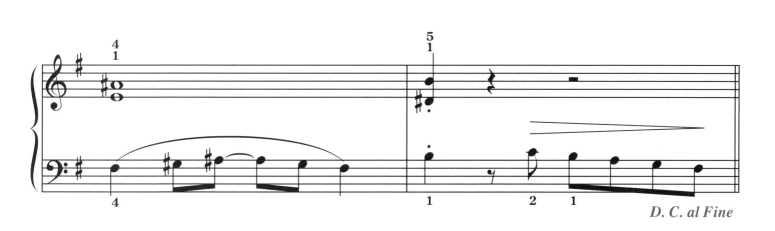

D. C. al Fine

STEAL AWAY

KEY OF D MAJOR
Key Signature: 2 sharps (F♯ & C♯)

COME BACK TO SORRENTO

This popular Neapolitan song has been a favorite selection for famous tenor soloists since the time of Caruso. It is often performed by Placido Domingo and Luciano Pavarotti.

Ernesto de Curtis

* Some pieces combine a minor key and its parallel major key. Parallel keys have the same *key-note*.
D minor and D major are *parallel* keys.

NOTE: You may now play Jeremiah Clarke's famous *TRUMPET TUNE,* on page 78 in the "AMBITIOUS" section of this book, if you wish!

In the Hall of the Mountain King
from "Peer Gynt Suite"

> **KEY OF B MINOR***
> Key Signature: 2 sharps (F♯ & C♯)

NOTE: This piece begins with *both* hands playing in bass clef!

Edvard Grieg

Alla marcia**

*REMINDER: B MINOR is the *relative minor* of the key of D MAJOR.

****Alla marcia** means "march-like."

*Note the spelling of the diminished 7th chord: D E♯ G♯ B. This means that it is an inversion of the E♯dim7:
E♯ G♯ B D. The correct spelling of any dim7 in root position skips one letter of the musical alphabet
between each note.

The A Major Scale

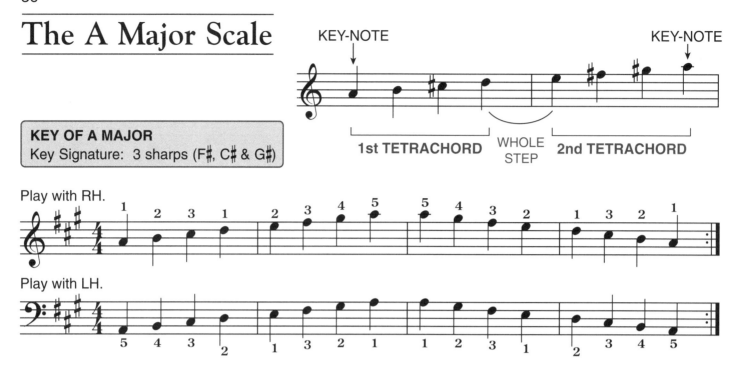

KEY OF A MAJOR
Key Signature: 3 sharps (F♯, C♯ & G♯)

Play with RH.

Play with LH.

THE A MAJOR SCALE IN CONTRARY MOTION

Practice this scale in parallel motion by playing the top two lines of this page with hands together.

AN AMERICAN HYMN

Many famous American composers, including Aaron Copland and Charles Ives, have made special arrangements of this 19th century hymn. This is a very quiet and contemplative setting.

Shall we gather at the river
Where bright angel feet have trod;
With its crystal tide forever
Flowing by the throne of God?

Yes, we'll gather at the river,
The beautiful, the beautiful river;
Gather with the saints at the river,
That flows by the throne of God.

Slowly and quietly

Robert Lowry

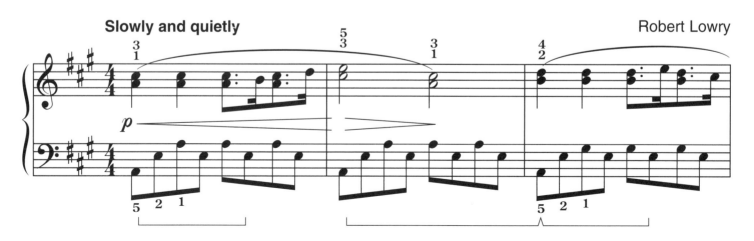

ADAGIO IN A MAJOR

This expressive piece is excellent preparation for the Chopin *PRELUDE IN A MAJOR,* found in the **"AMBITIOUS"** section on page 89.

Alexander Morovsky

* // = Caesura or pause.

The Key of F♯ Minor (Relative of A Major)

F♯ MINOR is the relative of A MAJOR. Both keys have the same key signature (3 sharps, F♯, C♯ & G♯).

THE F♯ HARMONIC MINOR SCALE

Play with RH.

THE F♯ HARMONIC MINOR SCALE IN CONTRARY MOTION

Practice this scale in parallel motion by playing the top two lines of this page with hands together.

The NATURAL & MELODIC MINOR scales may also be practiced in parallel and contrary motion.

• The NATURAL MINOR scale uses only the sharps in the key signature (no E♯).

• The MELODIC MINOR scale adds D♯ and E♯ ascending.
  The RH ascending fingering is 3 4 1 2 3 4 1 3. It descends like the natural minor.

BLUE RONDO*

Moderate blues tempo

Section Ⓐ

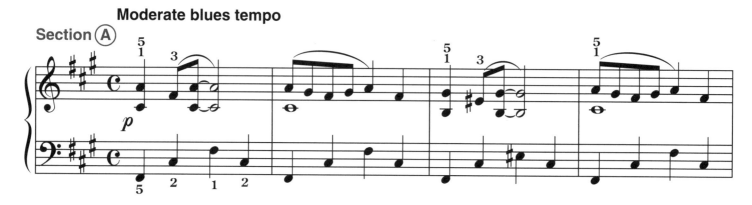

*A **rondo** has at least three sections. The first section is repeated after each of the other sections, and there is often a *CODA* (added ending).

Section B

Section A

Section C

Section A

Coda

The last two chords may be played
with *tremolo:*

The E Major Scale

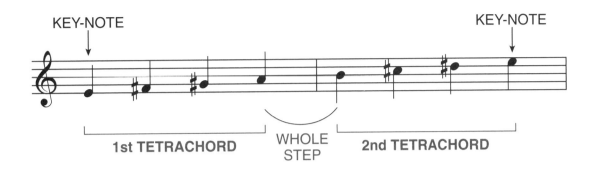

KEY-NOTE   KEY-NOTE

1st TETRACHORD   WHOLE STEP   2nd TETRACHORD

KEY OF E MAJOR
Key Signature: 4 sharps (F♯, C♯, G♯ & D♯)

Play with RH.

Play with LH.

THE E MAJOR SCALE IN CONTRARY MOTION

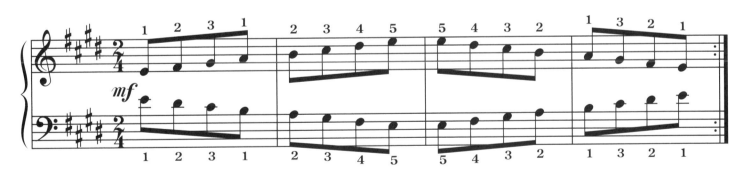

Practice this scale in parallel motion by playing the top two lines of this page with hands together.

LH Warm-up for *LAREDO*   *COUNT:*   1 & 2 & 3 & 4 &   1 & 2 & 3 & 4 &

Play several times, counting aloud.

LAREDO

This favorite Mexican folk song was used by the great American composer, Aaron Copland, as one of the themes in his famous symphonic composition, *El Salón Mexico.*

Traditional

Andante moderato

* ✕ Double sharp raises a sharped note one *half step,* or a natural note one *whole step.*

SHENANDOAH

American Folk Song

The Key of C♯ Minor (Relative of E Major)

C♯ MINOR is the relative of E MAJOR.

Both keys have the same key signature (4 sharps, F♯, C♯, G♯ & D♯).

THE C♯ HARMONIC MINOR SCALE

Play with RH.

Play with LH.

THE C♯ HARMONIC MINOR SCALE IN CONTRARY MOTION

Practice this scale in parallel motion by playing the top two lines of this page with hands together.

The NATURAL & MELODIC MINOR scales may also be practiced in parallel and contrary motion.

• The NATURAL MINOR scale uses only the sharps in the key signature (no B♯).

• The MELODIC MINOR scale uses A♯ and B♯ ascending.
  The RH ascending fingering is 3 4 1 2 3 4 1 3. It descends like the natural minor.

Jazz Ostinato* in C♯ Minor

This particular LH pattern is an excellent technical exercise!

Moderate blues tempo

Ostinato = Italian for "obstinate" or "persistent"; a pattern of notes repeated throughout the composition.

**Play the pairs of eighth notes a bit unevenly, long-short.

***The bass notes should fit with the first and third notes of the RH triplet.

NOTE: You may now begin to learn the first movement of Beethoven's famous *Moonlight Sonata,* if you wish.
It is found in the "AMBITIOUS" section of this book, on pages 90–93.

The E♭ Major Scale

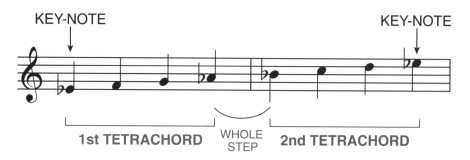

KEY OF E♭ MAJOR
Key Signature: 3 flats (B♭, E♭ & A♭)

After beginning with RH 3, the scale is fingered in groups of 1 2 3 4 – 1 2 3. End on 3.

After beginning with LH 3, the scale is fingered in groups of 3 2 1 – 4 3 2 1. End on 3.

THE E♭ MAJOR SCALE IN CONTRARY MOTION

Practice this scale in parallel motion by playing the top two lines of this page with hands together.

SOLDIER'S JOY (HORNPIPE)

Traditional

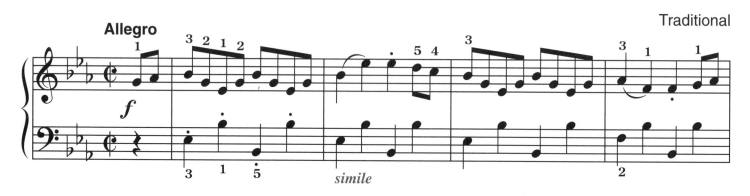

TOREADOR SONG from "Carmen"

George Bizet

*REMINDER: The three notes of a sixteenth-note triplet are played *evenly*, in the time of one EIGHTH NOTE.

The Key of C Minor (Relative of E♭ Major)

C MINOR is the relative of E♭ MAJOR.

Both keys have the same key signature (3 flats, B♭, E♭ & A♭).

THE C HARMONIC MINOR SCALE

Play with RH.

Play with LH.

THE C HARMONIC MINOR SCALE IN CONTRARY MOTION

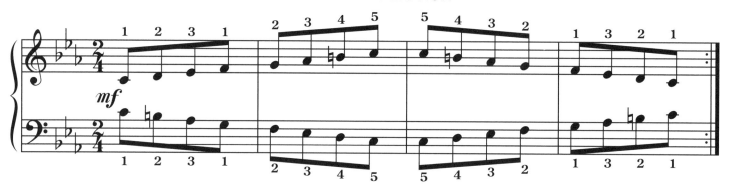

Practice this scale in parallel motion by playing the top two lines of this page with hands together.

The NATURAL & MELODIC MINOR scales may also be practiced in parallel and contrary motion. The fingering is the same.

The NATURAL MINOR scale uses only the flats in the key signature (no B♮).

The MELODIC MINOR scale uses A♮ and B♮ ascending.
It descends like the natural minor.

VARIATIONS ON A SEA CHANTY

Allegro moderato

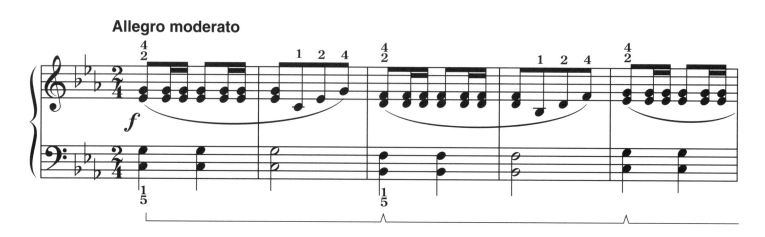

The A♭ Major Scale

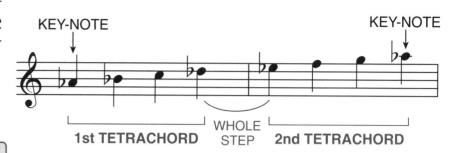

KEY-NOTE

KEY-NOTE

1st TETRACHORD — WHOLE STEP — 2nd TETRACHORD

KEY OF A♭ MAJOR
Key Signature: 4 flats (B♭, E♭, A♭ & D♭)

Play with RH.

Play with LH.

THE A♭ MAJOR SCALE IN CONTRARY MOTION

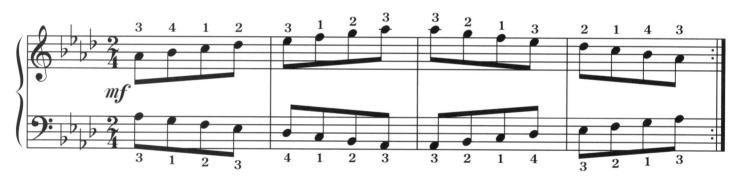

Practice this scale in parallel motion by playing the top two lines of this page with hands together.

DRY BONES

This piece will take you through the following major triads in all positions: A♭ major, A major, B♭ major, B major and C major. By using the suggestions at the bottom of the next page, you can use it to practice ALL the major triads!

Traditional

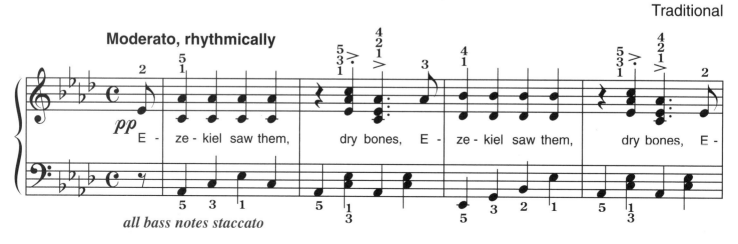

Moderato, rhythmically

pp

E - ze - kiel saw them, dry bones, E - ze - kiel saw them, dry bones, E -

all bass notes staccato

* Play the eighth notes in long-short pairs.

** To play ALL major triads in all positions, continue moving one half step up the keyboard every two measures until the 5th finger of the LH plays G. Use the following sequence of bones:

head, neck, shoulder, back, hip, thigh, knee, shin, leg, heel, foot, toe.

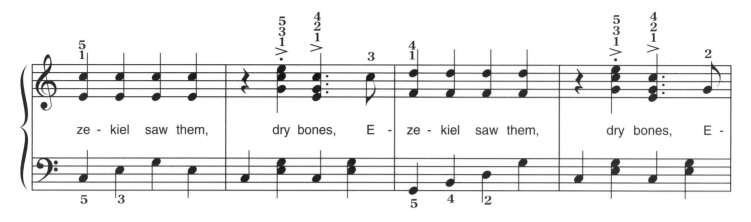

ze - kiel saw them, dry bones, E - ze - kiel saw them, dry bones, E -

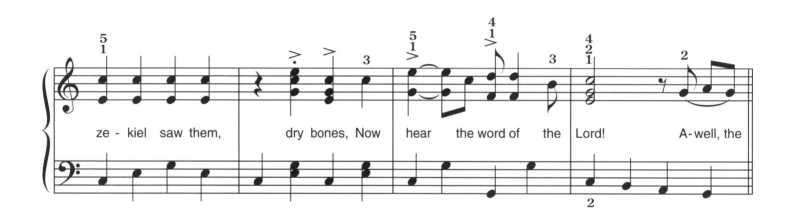

ze - kiel saw them, dry bones, Now hear the word of the Lord! A-well, the

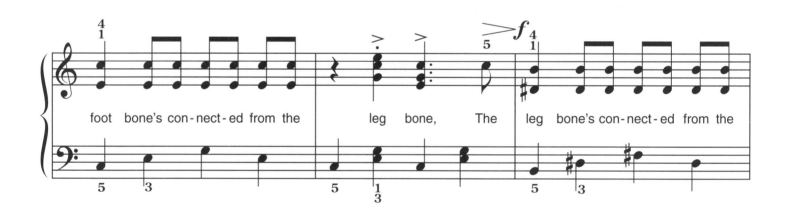

foot bone's con - nect - ed from the leg bone, The leg bone's con - nect - ed from the

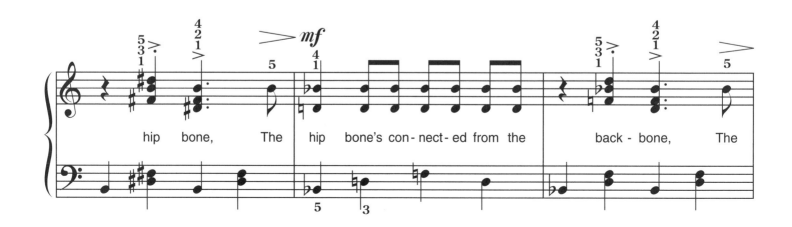

hip bone, The hip bone's con - nect - ed from the back - bone, The

COUNTRY SONG

Willard A. Palmer

Very slowly, with a gentle lilt

* Play the small note on the beat, together with the top note of the 3rd, then move rather quickly
  to the lower note of the 3rd. This produces a characteristic "country sound."

** Play the pairs of eighth notes long-short.

*REMINDER: *loco* means play as written (not *8va*).

"JUST FOR FUN" SECTION

This section (pages 62–73) contains pieces that are just a lot of fun to play! You may play from this section anytime you wish!

WHISTLIN' SAM

Andante moderato

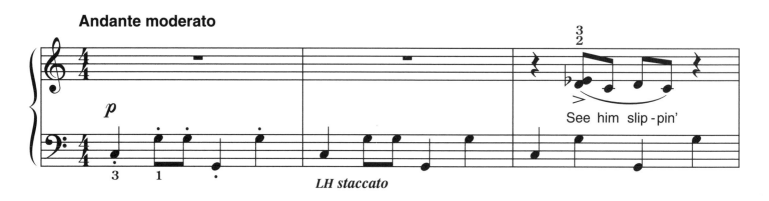

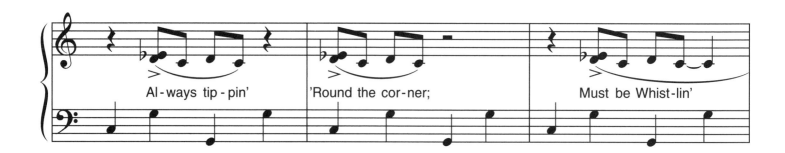

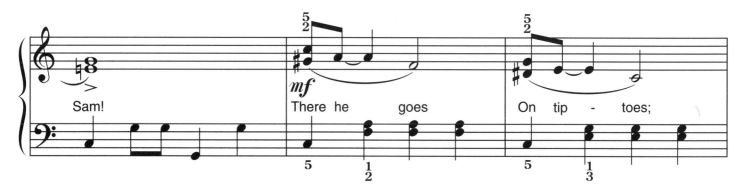

OPTIONAL: All pairs of eighth notes may be played long-short.

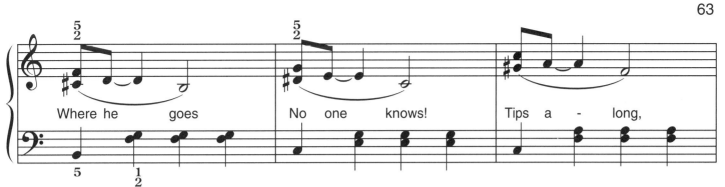

Where he goes No one knows! Tips a - long,

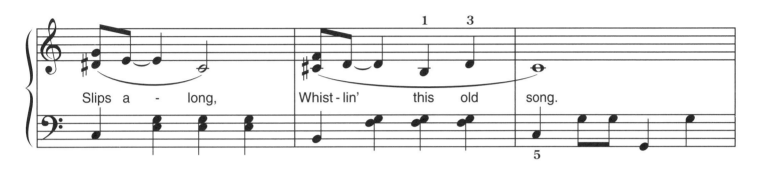

Slips a - long, Whist - lin' this old song.

p

(Vanishing away)

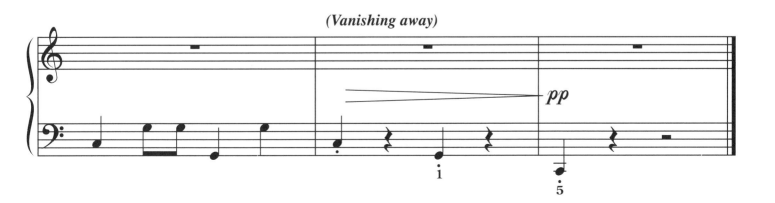

pp

JAZZ SEQUENCES*

Willard A. Palmer

Allegro moderato
2nd time both hands 8va

*The repetition of a musical pattern, beginning on a higher or lower note, is called a *sequence*.

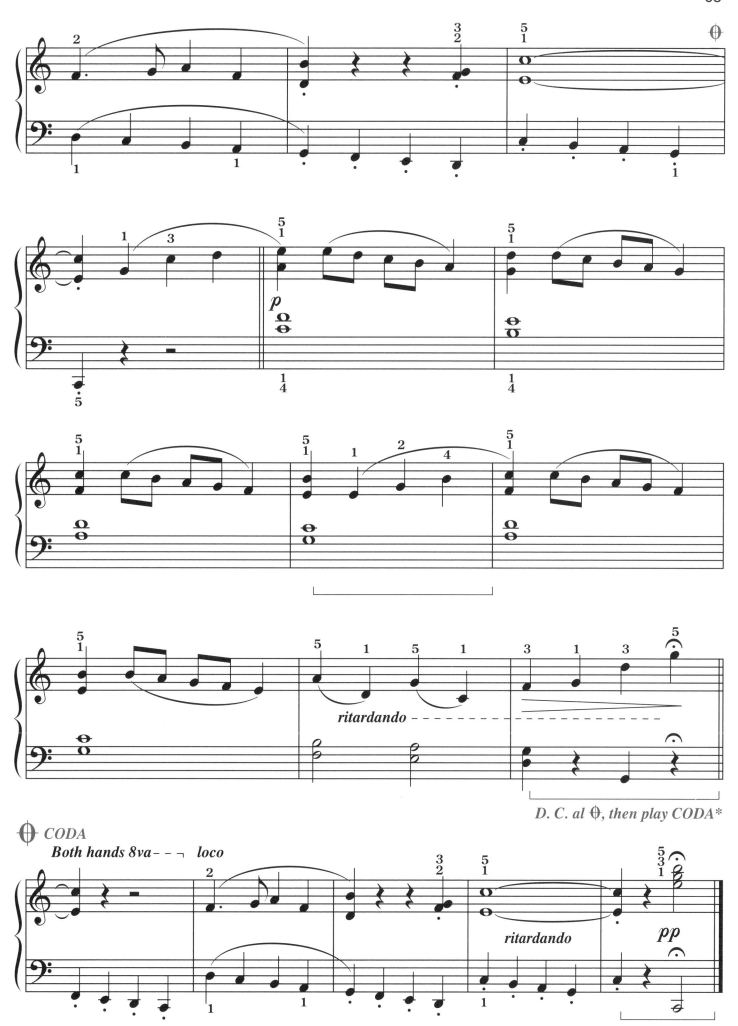

D. C. al $\oplus$, then play CODA*

$\oplus$ CODA

Both hands 8va - - - ⌐ loco

*Go back to the beginning and play to the sign $\oplus$; then play the CODA.

THE BIRTHSTONE BLUES

Bert Konowitz

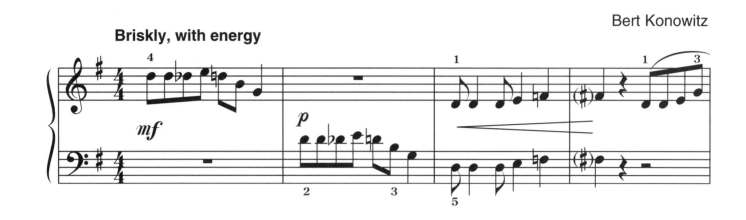

Play all pairs of eighth notes long-short.

This and the next page are from *Jazz Gems,* Book 1 (#14756), by Bert Konowitz.

68

THE GRAND PIANO BAND

March tempo
Eighths and quarters detached except where slurred.

Willard A. Palmer

*Play all eighth notes *evenly!*

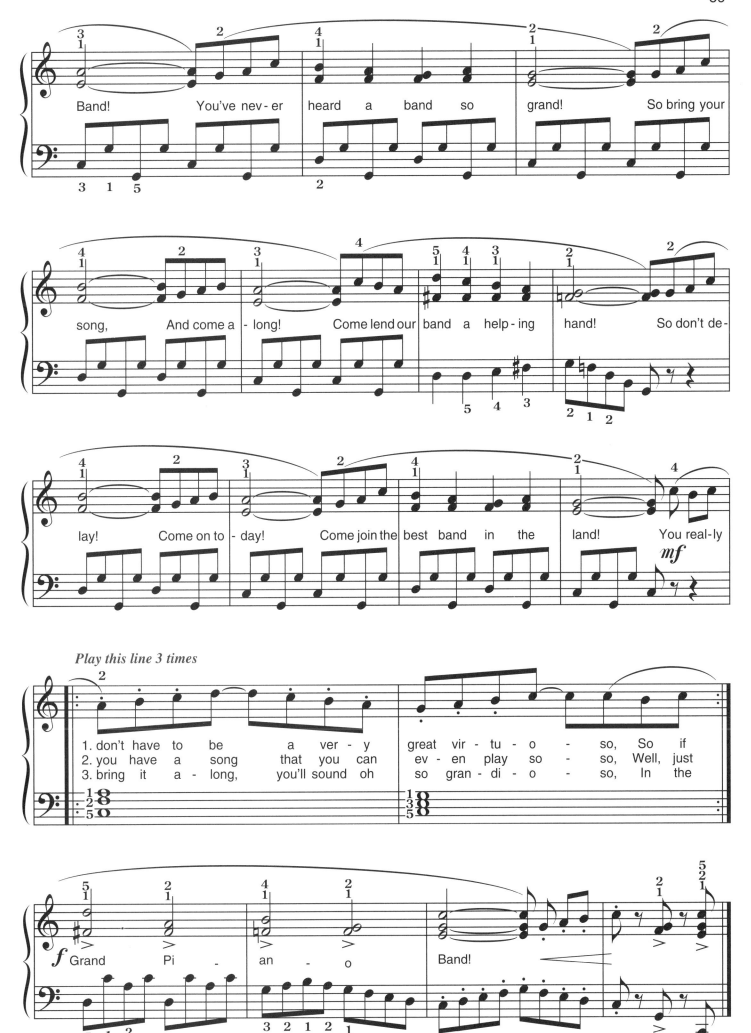

THE TAP-DANCER

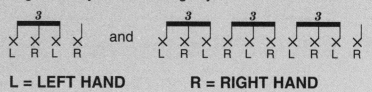

Extend the fingers of LH & RH, palms downward, to tap the rhythms indicated with x's on the wood *above* the fall-board. Or if you prefer, drum on your thighs. Only the following rhythms are used:

L = LEFT HAND   **R = RIGHT HAND**

Molto moderato (*not* fast!)
light and detached

Willard A. Palmer

D. S. 𝄋 al ⊕, then CODA

⊕ CODA

JUST A "GOOD OLD TUNE"

Happily
2nd time only, play both hands 8va

Willard A. Palmer

Not a rhap-so-dy and not a sym-pho-ny, It's just a sim-ple thing.

Not an in-ter-mez-zo, not a string quar-tet, So it's not

hard to sing. Makes me want to wig-gle, makes me

grin and gig-gle like some sil-ly loon!

Not a toc-ca-ta, not a so-na-ta, Just a good old tune!

*This piece is effective with eighth notes played evenly or with a slight lilt, *long-short*.

D. C. al ⊕, then CODA

CODA   Both hands 8va 1st time
       Both hands loco 2nd time

want to   wig - gle, makes me   grin and   gig - gle like some sil - ly   loon!

Not a toc-ca - ta,   not a so-na - ta,   Just   a   good old   tune!

Not a toc-ca - ta,   not a so-na - ta,   Just   a good old   tune! (Once more!)*   tune!

*Spoken: "Once more!"

"AMBITIOUS" Section

This section (pages 74 through 93) is included for those who would like to play well-known classics in their original form, and who are ambitious enough to apply a little extra effort to do so.

Each one of these pieces is possible for anyone who has carefully studied all of the preceding material, and who is willing to put in a little careful and patient practice. The results should be very satisfying!

PRELUDE IN C MAJOR
from "The Well-Tempered Clavier," Vol. 1

Andante con moto*

Johann Sebastian Bach

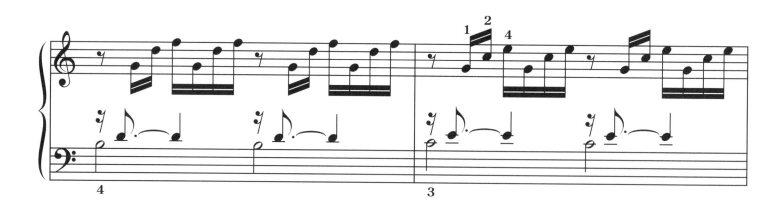

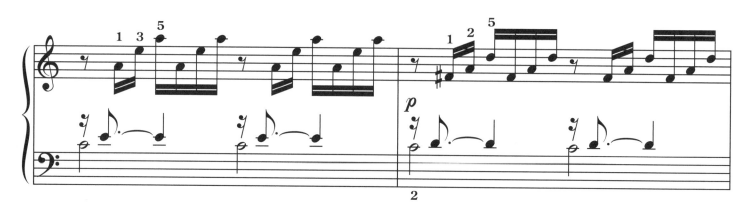

con moto means "with motion." Avoid holding back or dragging the tempo.

*Some editions have an extra measure added between this bar and the next. It is incorrect, and is not found in any of J. S. Bach's manuscripts or those of his family members.

77

TRUMPET TUNE

This piece, played at many festive occasions and often used as a wedding march, is sometimes attributed to the great English composer, Henry Purcell. It was actually composed by one of his friends, Jeremiah Clarke (c. 1673–1707).

Alla marcia

Jeremiah Clarke

Thirty-Second Notes

When one thirty-second note is written alone, it looks like this:

Thirty-second notes are usually written:

in pairs,   or in groups of four,   or in groups of eight.

Eight thirty-second notes are played in the time of one quarter note.

There can be 32 thirty-second notes in one measure of COMMON (4/4) TIME!

Play several times—first ADAGIO, then ANDANTE, then ALLEGRO MODERATO.

Four thirty-second notes are played in the time of one eighth note.

Play several times—first ADAGIO, then ANDANTE, then ALLEGRO MODERATO.

Toccata in D Minor

This piano transcription of the toccata from one of J. S. Bach's most famous organ works, *TOCCATA AND FUGUE IN D MINOR*, is not a simplification. All of the notes of the original are included.

Johann Sebastian Bach

*Pairs of eighths within the triplet pattern are played long-short to accommodate them to the basic triplet rhythm, according to the practice of the period. (This applies only to measures 6–14.)

Allegro moderato

Molto maestoso

Pesante means "heavy." Play each note with great firmness and emphasis.

Preparation for *FÜR ELISE*   This piece, dedicated to a girl named *Elise* in 1810, is one of the most popular of all masterworks. The following measures contain unusual crossings of the LH 2nd finger over the thumb. Play the ¾ measures first. Begin slowly, gradually increasing speed, then play the ⅜ measures.

FÜR ELISE

Ludwig van Beethoven

Poco moto*

Moto means "motion."   **Poco moto** means "moving along a bit," or "rather fast."

**The pedal indications, derived from the original edition, have been adapted to the greater resonance of the modern piano and for modern "overlapping pedal" techniques.

***Most editions have D instead of E. The original edition and the only known fragmentary Beethoven manuscript both have E, as shown above.

* ·‿· The dots over or under the slurs indicate *portato*, sometimes called *mezzo staccato*.
   The notes are only slightly separated (long but detached).
** Play the small notes very quickly, on the beat of the following large note.

* Note Beethoven's spelling of the diminished 7th chord: E G B♭ C♯. This means that it is an inversion
   of the C♯dim7: C♯ E G B♭. The correct spelling of any diminished 7th in root position skips one letter
   of the musical alphabet between each note.

* This chord is a G♯dim7 with the 3rd (B) omitted.

** In the original edition, the pedal is held from here to the end of the page. The resonance of the modern piano makes this impractical, in the opinion of the editors.

PRELUDE IN A MAJOR

Frédéric Chopin
Op. 28, No. 7

*This chord may be divided between the hands
as follows. Play the small notes very quickly.
(The composer did not indicate the wavy line.)

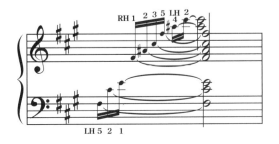

SONATA QUASI UNA FANTASIA

"Moonlight Sonata" (First Movement)

When Beethoven's *SONATA QUASI UNA FANTASIA* (Sonata in the Style of a Fantasy) was first performed, a critic wrote that the first movement reminded him of "moonlight on Lake Lucerne." The public named it "Moonlight Sonata," and it is probably the most popular of Beethoven's piano works.

Ludwig van Beethoven
Op. 27, No. 2

Adagio sostenuto*

***Sostenuto** means "sustaining the tone."

Beethoven's instructions at the beginning of this piece are as follows:

> *This entire piece must be played very delicately and without dampers.*

The instruction "without dampers" was used on pieces written when the dampers were lifted by a knee lever rather than by a pedal. It means that the dampers should be off the strings. This is the same as our modern instructions to USE THE PEDAL. Thus "without dampers" = with pedal.

Modern pedal indications are added by the editors.

Dictionary of Musical Terms

Accelerando . . . . gradually increasing in speed

Accent sign (>) . . . . play with special emphasis

Adagio . . . . slow

Alla marcia . . . . in the style of a march, or "march-like"

Allargando . . . . becoming slower and broader

Allegretto . . . . rather fast; a little slower than *allegro*

Allegro . . . . quickly, happily, fast

Andante . . . . moving along (walking speed)

Animato . . . . animated; lively

Appoggiatura (♪ or ♪) . . a small ornamental note. Its purpose is to add expression to the melody.

Arpeggio . . . . a chord played in a "harp-like" fashion, broken or rolled

A tempo . . . . resume original speed

Atonal . . . . not in any definite key

Cantabile . . . . in a singing style

Coda . . . . an added ending

Coda sign (⊕) . . . . indication to proceed to *Coda,* which usually has the same sign

Common time (𝐂) . . . . . . same as $\frac{4}{4}$ time

Con brio . . . . with vigor or brilliance

Con moto . . . . with motion (moving along)

Con spirito . . . . with spirit

Contrary motion . . . . hands moving in opposite directions

Crescendo (◁) . . . . . gradually louder

Da Capo al Fine . . . . repeat from the beginning to the word "Fine"

Dal Segno al Fine . . . . . . repeat from the sign 𝄋 to the word "Fine"

Development . . . . the part of a composition in which the main themes (subjects) are
treated with freedom and imagination

Diminuendo (▷) . . . . gradually softer

Dolce . . . . sweetly

Double flat (♭♭) . . . . lowers a flatted note one *half* step, or a natural note one *whole* step

Double sharp (𝄪) . . . . raises a sharped note one *half* step, or a natural note one *whole* step

Elision . . . . when one slur ends just as another begins on the same note

Espressivo . . . . expressively

Exposition . . . . the first statement of the main theme or themes of a composition

Fermata (⌢) . . . . hold the note or notes under the sign longer

Fine . . . . the end

Forte (*f*) . . . . loud

Fortissimo (*ff*) . . . . very loud

Grandioso . . . . in a grand and majestic manner

Grazioso . . . . gracefully

Interval . . . . the distance from one note to the next

Largo . . . . very slow

Legato . . . . smoothly connected

Leggiero . . . . lightly

Loco . . . . as written (not *8va*)

Maestoso . . . . majestically

Meno mosso . . . . slower

Mezzo forte (*mf*) . . . . moderately loud

Mezzo piano (*mp*) . . . . . . moderately soft

Moderato . . . . a moderate speed

Molto . . . . much, very

Mordent (⌾) . . . . an ornament that alternates the written note with the tone below.
It is played quickly: written note, lower note, written note.

Morendo . . . . dying away

Moto . . . . motion

Octave sign (*8va*) . . . . play 8 scale tones (one octave) higher when the sign is above the notes;
8 scale tones lower when the sign is below the notes

Parallel motion . . . . hands moving in the same direction

Pesante . . . . heavy

Pianissimo (*pp*) . . . . very soft

Piano (*p*) . . . . soft

Più . . . . more

Più *f* . . . . louder

Più mosso . . . . faster

Poco . . . . little, small

Poco a poco . . . . little by little

Poco moto . . . . moving along a bit; rather fast

Polytonal . . . . in two or more keys at the same time

Portato . . . . a manner of playing between legato & staccato, sometimes called
mezzo staccato. The notes are only slightly separated (long but detached).

Prestissimo . . . . very fast

Presto . . . . fast

Recapitulation . . . . a repetition of the main theme or themes of a piece, after a development
or other section has been heard

Repeat sign (▤) . . . . repeat from the beginning, or from ▤

Risoluto . . . . resolutely, boldly

Ritardando . . . . gradually slowing

Ritenuto . . . . literally "holding back." Slowing down the tempo immediately.

Scherzo . . . . a musical joke

Segue . . . . continue

Sequence . . . . repetition of a musical pattern, beginning on a higher or lower note

Sforzando (*sf*) . . . . forcing; suddenly loud on one note or chord

Simile . . . . continue in the same manner

Sostenuto . . . . sustaining the tone

Staccato . . . . short, detached

Tempo . . . . rate of speed

Tenuto (−) . . . . hold for full value; emphasize slightly

Tetrachord . . . . 4 tones having a pattern of *whole step—whole step—half step*

Theme . . . . a complete musical idea or subject

Tonal . . . . in a definite key

Tranquillo . . . . calm; tranquil

Triad . . . . a three-note chord: root, 3rd, 5th

Trill (⌾ or *tr*) . . . . an ornament that alternates the written note with the
next scale tone above, several or many times

Vivace . . . . lively; faster than *allegro,* but slower than *presto*

Certificate of Award

This is to certify that

_____

has successfully completed

Alfred's Basic Adult Piano Course, Level 3.

_____
Date

_____
Teacher